# YOUR KNOWLEDGE HAS VALUE

- We will publish your bachelor's and master's thesis, essays and papers

- Your own eBook and book - sold worldwide in all relevant shops

- Earn money with each sale

Upload your text at www.GRIN.com
and publish for free

**Bibliographic information published by the German National Library:**

The German National Library lists this publication in the National Bibliography; detailed bibliographic data are available on the Internet at http://dnb.dnb.de .

**Imprint:**

Copyright © 2017 GRIN Verlag, Open Publishing GmbH
Print and binding: Books on Demand GmbH, Norderstedt Germany
ISBN: 9783668459885

**This book at GRIN:**

http://www.grin.com/en/e-book/366933/introduction-into-game-theory-business-context

Mike G.

# Introduction into Game Theory (Business Context)

GRIN Publishing

**GRIN - Your knowledge has value**

Since its foundation in 1998, GRIN has specialized in publishing academic texts by students, college teachers and other academics as e-book and printed book. The website www.grin.com is an ideal platform for presenting term papers, final papers, scientific essays, dissertations and specialist books.

**Visit us on the internet:**

http://www.grin.com/

http://www.facebook.com/grincom

http://www.twitter.com/grin_com

# Introduction into Game Theory

From the popular series "Numb3rs" you may know the term "Game Theory", but do you actually know what this is and how it works? During a six-week session of microeconomics, several basic principles are introduces and applied in the business context. Game Theory deals with the optimal behavior of rational decision makers in a simplified surrounding. This text deals with the optimal behavior during a second price action and within oligopolistic competition. The basic ideas like the prisoner's dilemma are explained and underlined with real examples to simplify and illustrate the dry mathematics behind it. After reading this text, you will be able to solve certain problems in a simplified surrounding by your own and will perceive the world at least a little bit more rational.

- **Introduction into Game Theory.**
- Goals of game theory are
- Analysis of strategic interactions (competition between companies).
- Prediction of human behavior and market outcome.
- Determine rational behavior.
- Game is strategic interaction between rational players with conflicting interests.
- Blue-prints of a game description.

| Players | Amount of involved players |
|---------|----------------------------|
| Rules | Actions, timing and information |
| Outcomes | Predict outcome of each set of actions |
| Payoffs | Player's preferences |

- Subsequent or simultaneous timing?
- Who knows which information and when?
- Pay attention on the following points.
- Actions: Don't have to e numerical (e.g., "advertise" or "not advertise").

| Element | Description |
|---------|-------------|
| Players | • 2 players, e.g., one student, one lecturer |
| Rules | • actions: stone (st), scissor (sc), paper (pa)<br>• timing: decisions are made simultaneously<br>• information: each player knows the rules of the game and the other player's preferences; since moves are simultaneously, no player knows the action choice of her opponent |
| Outcomes | • (st,sc) -> first player wins<br>• (st,st) -> draw<br>• (st,pa) -> second player wins<br>• … |
| Payoffs | • Both players prefer winning to a draw to loosing |

- Practical example: Stone – Scissor – Paper

- **First mover vs. late mover.**
- First mover advantages are psychological standards (consumers taste is related to your

product), a higher share of loyal consumers, and higher valued products.
- Late mover advantages are learning from mistakes of the first mover, chance to redefine the product category by innovation, low imitation costs (save money for research and development).

- **Static Games with discrete payoffs (simultaneous actions).**
- **Prisoner's Dilemma.**
- Creation of a static payoff matrix.

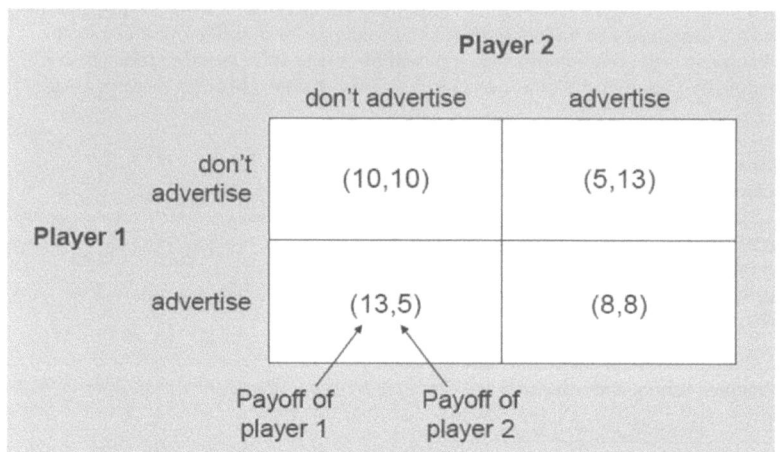

- To find the optimal outcome (and action of both players) we have to find the Nash equilibrium.
- Assume player two decides for "advertise", how will player one will react rationally?
- Answer this questions in every differentiation and find the solution preferred by both.
→ In this case "advertise" is the best option for both players irrespective how the other player decides.
- We say "strategy "advertise" dominates the strategy "don't advertise"" (and v.v.).
- **Problem / Characteristic of the prisoner's dilemma.**
- If both decide not do do the action, they will be better-off.
- But if this is the case, both have strong incentive to do the action and become even better.
=> Lack of information, trust and certainty leads to a lower, but safer outcome.
- **The original construction around the prisoner's dilemma.**
- Police arrested two suspects in a serious crime, but only can prove a small crime.
- Interrogate both simultaneously separated from each other and both will confess doing the crime together with the partner.
=> Both will receive the highest penalty because of strong incentive to confess.

- **Specifics on Nash equilibrium.**
- If there are more than one Nash equilibria, no dominant strategy is existing.

- Even if player 2 has no dominant strategy, he consider the dominant strategy of player 1 and rationally react to it.

## Games with discrete payoffs

|          | Player 2 A | Player 2 B |
|----------|------------|------------|
| **Player 1** a | (1,10)     | (1,13)     |
| **Player 1** b | (3,4)      | (2,3)      |

## A different game

no dominated strategies

|          | Player 2 A | Player 2 B |
|----------|------------|------------|
| **Player 1** a | (1,3)      | (2,4)      |
| **Player 1** b | (2,2)      | (0,1)      |

- **Static Games with continuous payoffs.**
- No longer distinguish "do" or "do not", now consider e.g. how much has to be invested.
- We have to set up the profit (or utility) function of both players and prove the first order condition to identify where they have no incentive to change.
- **Numerical Example: Advertising Game.**
- Symmetric firms, each firm can choose whether to invest into advertisement or not.
- Advertisement costs are $a_i{}^2$ with $i = 1, 2$
- No other costs, demand is limited, has to be stolen from the competitor.
- Price for the products equals 1.
- Demand function of company 1 $D_1 = 1 + a_1 - \frac{1}{2} * a_2 - a_1 * a_2$
- Profit function of company 1 $\pi_1 = 1 + a_1 - \frac{1}{2} * a_2 - a_1 * a_2 - a_1^2$
- First order condition reveals $\pi_{1a_1} = 1 - a_2 - 2a_1 \rightarrow a_1 = \frac{1-a_2}{2}$

→ Best response function of company 1.
- $a_1$ is negatively responding to $a_2$ therefore the slope is negative (falling reaction curve).
=> Strategic substitutes.
- Because of two symmetric companies the demand and profit function for company 2 equals those of company 1 (only with switched indices).
- Inserting both variables into the other formula will reveal $a_1{}^* = a_2{}^* = 1/3$
=> Nash equilibrium (invest 33% of one million or the

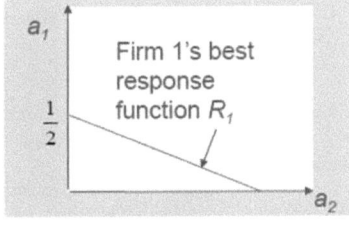

Firm 1's best response function $R_1$

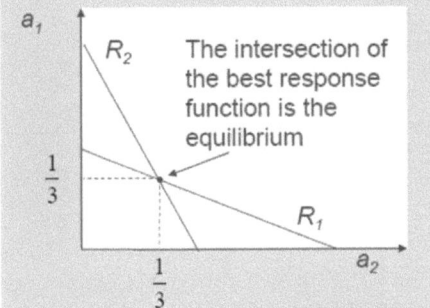

The intersection of the best response function is the equilibrium

respected unit).

3

- **Zero-sum games and mixed strategies.**
- Explained by the "Matching Pennies" example.
- Two players have one euro coin each and choose either to face head or tail up and simultaneously they will display their choice.
- If both coins sides match, player 2 receives the coin from player 1 and v.v.
- Creating the payoff matrix will lead to no Nash equilibrium.

=> Pure strategies fail to exist.

|  | Heads Player 2 Tails | |
|---|---|---|
| **Heads** Player 1 | (-1,1) | (1,-1) |
| **Tails** | (1,-1) | (-1,1) |

- Directly conflicting interest are the reason:

For each choice the other player does, we have incentive to do it different.
- Find out if opting for one decision is more likely to win or not (e.g. related to the preferences of the other player).
- So far we calculated with possibilities that will occur ($p = 1$) or which aren't related to our optimal choice; now we deal with real possibilities ($p \leq 1$).
- To opt for a random choice must be the optimal reaction to the random choice of the opponent.
- To make this possible, all possibilities of player 2 must reveal the same yield irrespective to the decision player 1 will do.

=> Find a situation for this to hold and you can calculate the optimal choice of player 1 as well as the expected equilibrium outcome.
- Formalize the payoff of player 2 from choosing heads if q is the probability of player 1 to

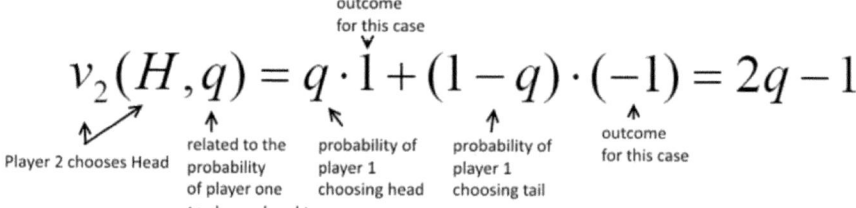

outcome for this case

$$v_2(H,q) = q \cdot 1 + (1-q) \cdot (-1) = 2q - 1$$

Player 2 chooses Head | related to the probability of player one to choose head too | probability of player 1 choosing head | probability of player 1 choosing tail | outcome for this case

choose head and p the related one for player 2.
- Do the same for tails and equalize both equations which reveals $q = \frac{1}{2}$.
- Do the same for player one and you will receive $p = \frac{1}{2}$.
- If q is greater than $\frac{1}{2}$ player 2 should prefer Head over Tail and v.v.
- Player 1 will mix choices with probability of 50%, so for player 2 the rational reaction is to choose between both mixes with 50% probability.
- *In the exam: Underline each rational reaction in the strategic form representation and make two lines between nod and outcome in the extensive form representation to show your way of thoughts.*

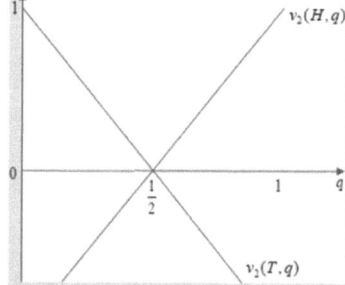

- **Sequential Games (actions are followed by each other).**
  - Explained by the Market Entry Game example.
  - If supposing simultaneous decisions two Nash equilibria will occur.
=> Neither A nor B have a dominant strategy.
  - In case of sequential games, player A can identify the rational reaction of B on his own decisions, therefore choose more wisely.
  - To show this sequential decision making process, the concept of Nash equilibrium has to be redefined.
  - First of all we change the "strategic form representation" into an "extensive form representation" to show the sequence.
  - With this "decision tree" we can determine the best (= rational) reaction of player B on player A's decision.
=> Same solution like in case of simultaneous decision making process ((0,2); (2,0)).
  - Rational analysis reveals that (0,2) is an implausible equilibrium, to reflect this way of thought in our model, we have to introduce another concept.
  - **Subgame Perfect Equilibria (SPE).**
  - Each decision node (two or more possible choices) constitutes a subgame.
  - We will reduce the decision tree to reveal the best decision of player A by shorting each subgame down to the one and only rational decision of player B.
  - Important is "backward induction" (otherwise the SPE isn't working), start with the latest (in term of stages) decision node and find the best response.
Than reduce both nodes to the optimal reaction and determine the choice of A.

Strategic Form Representation

|        |        | **B** enter | don't   |
|--------|--------|-------------|---------|
| **A**  | enter  | (-1,-1)     | (2,0)   |
|        | don't  | (0,2)       | (0,0)   |

This game has two NE

Extensive Form Representation

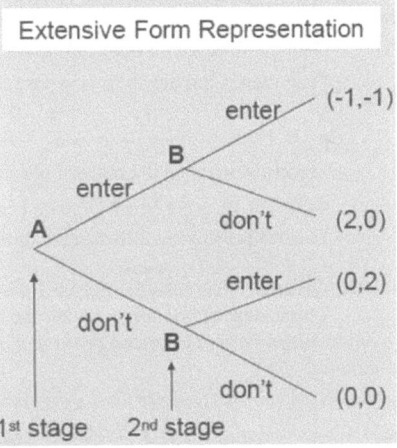

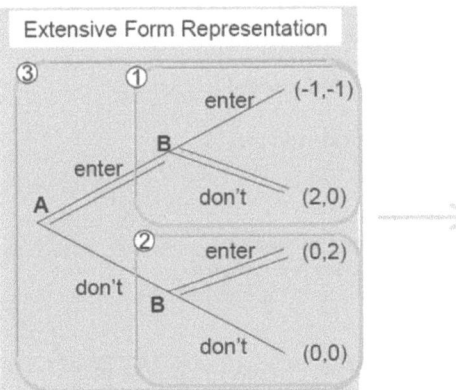

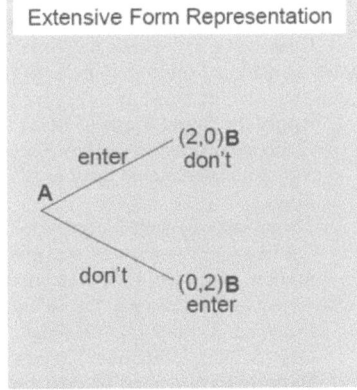

=> Now we can see that our model of SPE delivers the correct answer, (2,0) is the only subgame perfect equilibrium.

5

- In the exam: Always distinguish the type of equilibria (pure strategies (Nash equilibrium), mixed strategies (in case of zero-sum games), subgame perfect equilibrium (SPE)).
- **Distinction between action and strategy.**
- In our static game examples actions equals strategy.
- In sequential games only for the first-mover action equals strategy.
- Follower has a strategy, i.e. a plan of actions related to the decision the first mover did.
=> Strategy as contingent plan.
- A has two possible strategies, B has four which are related to the decision A makes.
→ Number of possible strategies equals $a^d$ with a = number of actions; d = number of decision nodes.

- **Sequential game with continuous actions.**
- Advertisement game, how much money should be invested into advertisement?
- Two companies in the market competing about market shares, can increase this with advertisement.
- Company 1 is the first mover and company 2 will follow, what are the optimal marketing budgets and has company 1 a first-mover advantage?
- Demand function of both symmetric firms $D = 1 + a_2 - \frac{1}{2} * a_1 - a_2 * a_1$
- **First step**: Find the "best response function" of follower by first derivative of profit function.
- $\pi_2 = 1 + a_2 - \frac{1}{2} * a_1 - a_2 * a_1 - a_2^2 \pi_2' = 1 - a_1 - 2a_2 \rightarrow a_2 = \frac{1-a_1}{2}$
- **Second step**: Find the optimal choice of first mover by inserting $a_2$ into profit function.
- $\pi_1 = 1 + a_1 - \frac{1}{2} * \left(\frac{1-a_1}{2}\right) - a_1 * \left(\frac{1-a_1}{2}\right) - a_1^2 \pi_1' = 1 + \frac{1}{4} - \frac{1}{2} + a_1 - 2a_1$
- This leads us to the following results: $a_1* = \frac{3}{4} > a_1*$ simultaneous $= 1/3$
- $a_2* = 1/8 < a_2*$ simultaneous $= 1/3$
=> The advertisement costs for player 1 have increased since she becomes the first-mover.
- **Third step**: Determine whether the leader has a first-mover advantage or not.
- Comparison of expected profit in case of simultaneous decision making process and sequential one.
- $\pi_1 *. (simultaneous) = \pi_2 *. (simultaneous) = 1 + \frac{1}{3} - \frac{1}{2} * \frac{1}{3} - \frac{1}{3} * \frac{1}{3} - \frac{1}{9} = \frac{17}{8} \approx 0.94$
- $\pi_1 *. (sequential) = \frac{7}{4} - \frac{1}{16} - \frac{3}{32} - \frac{9}{16} = \frac{33}{32} \approx 1.03$
- $\pi_2 *. (sequentail) = \frac{9}{8} - \frac{3}{8} - \frac{3}{32} - \frac{1}{64} = \frac{41}{64} \approx 0.64$
=> Because $\pi_1*$ (sequential) is greater than $\pi_1*$ (simultaneous) player 1 has a first-mover advantage.
- Advantage is related to the fact that advertisement is a **strategic substitute**.
- If one company spends more money for advertisement, than the other company faces decreasing marginal revenue in investing too, so it has incentive to spend less money.

- **Apply the foundations of game theory in a practical example.**
- **Game characteristics of an Second Price Auction.**
- *Players*: infinite large number n.
- *Rules.*:
- *Timing*: simultaneously, but with the chance to adjust your decision.
- *Information*: valuation of the object by the other players is not known.
- *Actions*: Make a bid with the hope to receive the object. If you are the highest bidder you win the object and have to pay the second highest bid.
- *Outcomes*: Continuous variables.
- *Payoffs*: Win the auction, but pay less than the valuation to receive a salary (x-p)/2.
- **Hypothesis to prove**: The unique pure strategy equilibrium is $b_i* = x_i$
→ Prove by exclusion (i.e. show that in case of $b_i \neq x_i$ you could have been better off if adjusting

the bid closer to $x_i$ ).

- 1) First possible situation: $b_i > x_i$

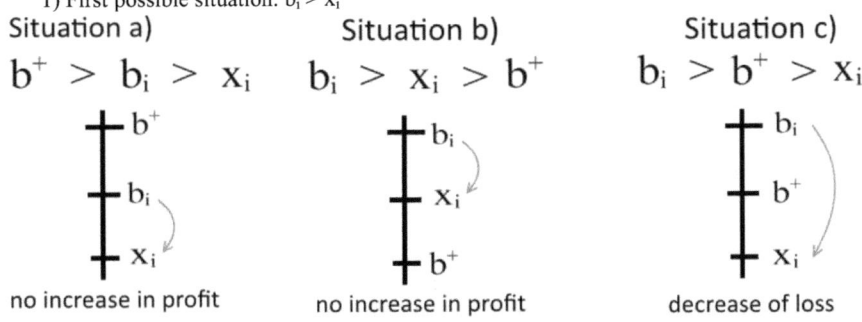

| Situation a) | Situation b) | Situation c) |
|---|---|---|
| $b^+ > b_i > x_i$ | $b_i > x_i > b^+$ | $b_i > b^+ > x_i$ |
| no increase in profit | no increase in profit | decrease of loss -> increase of profit |

- Conclusions: in the case of a) and b) you're totally indifferent whether to decrease the price or not; in case of c) adjust the bid closer to $x_i$ to lose the auction and face no profit instead of a loss. $\Pi = (x_i - b^+) < 0$

- 2) Second possible situation: $x_i > b_i$

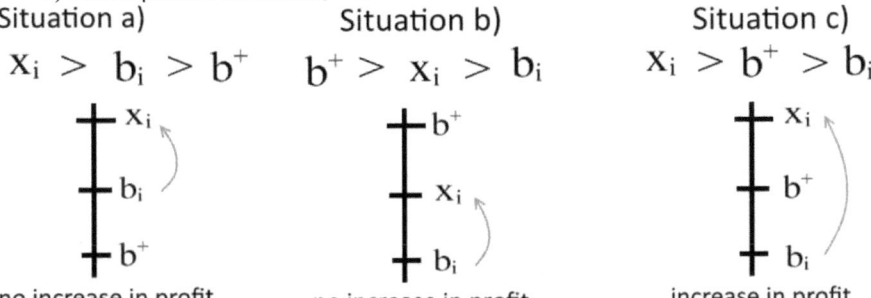

| Situation a) | Situation b) | Situation c) |
|---|---|---|
| $x_i > b_i > b^+$ | $b^+ > x_i > b_i$ | $x_i > b^+ > b_i$ |
| no increase in profit | no increase in profit | increase in profit |

- Conclusions: In case of c) adjusting the bid to $x_i$ will make you win the auction and receive a salary. $\Pi = (x_i - b^+) > 0$

=> Nash equilibrium in dominant strategies is $x_i = b_i$ .

- **Oligopolistic competition.**
- Pure monopoly and perfect competition are rare in reality, oligopolistic market structures are more common because most companies have at least a little bit of market power.
→ They have to take both into account, the behavior of consumers as well as of competitors.
- Several dimensions of oligopolistic competition, e.g., location, branding, price and quantity.
→ The last two are the most important and are explained in more detail in the following.
- *First assumption* is that the market sells homogeneous products like oil or grain.

- **General information about the market.**
- *Demand side*: Many consumers, all are price takers, have no market power.
- *Supply side*: assumption of homogeneous goods provided by only a few companies.
- **Different (less known) market types.**
- Bilateral bargaining: One seller meets one buyer (e.g. in case of technology research).
- Oligopsony: Many sellers meet only a few buyers (e.g. grocery).
- Monopsony: Many sellers meet only one buyer (e.g. labor market).
- Company hires workers, limits the total amount of vacancy to create artificial shortage and decrease the salary; Workers "sell" their time and effort to the company.

- **Famous market types explained with examples.**
- Monopoly: Patent protected drugs are only provided by one seller, but many buyers existing needing the drug → seller as price setter.
- Oligopoly: Company can affect the market price, but has to be aware that consumers go to the competitor.
- Perfect competition: The market for milk is very large and many farmers take the price for granted, increase or decrease in quantity supplied won't affect the market at all.

- **Timing of strategic decisions.**
- Most difficult task in an oligopoly is to anticipate what the competitor will do.
- Therefore different timings have to be distinguished.
- **(1) Simultaneous moves (e.g., mobile tariffs).**
- Special Christmas offer of a mobile service provider has to be better than the competitors, but have to be prepared simultaneously with the opponents.
- **(2) Sequential moves (e.g., gasoline prices).**
- Observe the strategic decisions (price decisions) of your opponent and adjust your decision.
- **(3) Repeated interaction (e.g., short-term lending rates).**
- Banks will constitute an interest rate for short-term credits every morning. Because it is a repeated action there won't be price pressure and one price will be stabilized.

- **Strategic Variables.**
- Strategic decisions are called strategic variables.
- **Price**: Consumers like the cheapest prices.
- **Quantities**: Influencing the quantity supplied will influence the price and quantity demanded.
- **Product differentiation**: Different styles (horizontal) or quality (vertical).
- **Location**: Different accessibility determines demand.
- **Information**: Information provided will influence the demand (eco awards).

- **Strategic interactions can be distinguished by strategic variables and timing.**
- *Bertrand* competition (simultaneous moves, prices).
- *Cournot* competition (simultaneous moves, quantities).
- *Bertrand-Stackelberg* (sequential moves, price).
- *Cournot-Stackelberg* (sequential moves, quantities).

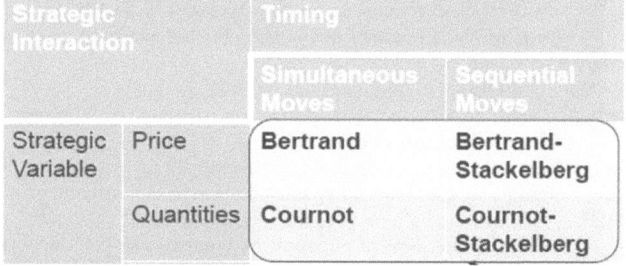

| Strategic Interaction | | Timing | |
|---|---|---|---|
| | | **Simultaneous Moves** | **Sequential Moves** |
| Strategic Variable | Price | Bertrand | Bertrand-Stackelberg |
| | Quantities | Cournot | Cournot-Stackelberg |

- **Bertrand Paradox.**
- **Assumptions**.
- Single market with homogeneous products, symmetric firms, consumers only buy for the cheapest price, if the same price than equal demand split, no capacity constraints.
- Costs of both firms $C_1 = c * q_1$    $C_2 = c * q_2$
- **Hypothesis.**
- The equilibrium is said to be $p_1 = p_2 = c$.
- **Prove.**
- Best choice of company 1 if company 2 chooses $p_2 = c$ is $p_1 = c$.
- If $p_2 > c$, than company 1 has incentive to lower the price as much / often as possible (until p = c).

- No other equilibrium than this one.
- In the equilibrium the profit of each firm is $\pi_{all} = \frac{1}{2} * D(p) * (p - c)$
- Consider company 2 lowers the price by m, then $\pi_2 = D(p - m) * (p - m - c)$
- Such a decrease in price is always possible if $\frac{1}{2} * D(p) * (p - c) < D(p - m) * (p - m - c) \rightarrow \frac{D(p)}{2D(p-m)} < \frac{p-m-c}{p-c}$
- If $m \rightarrow \infty$, than the term above equals $\frac{1}{2} < 1$ which is always true.

=> Because the cost can't be undercut, the optimal price of both companies is p = MC.

- **Conclusions.**
- Positive: Realistic behavioral assumptions (firms set the price, customers only care about the price).
- Negative: The outcome seems unrealistic because it is the same like in pure competition.

$\rightarrow$ Related to the assumption of free capacity; in reality companies examine their optimal quantity and than calculate the price.

- **Cournot Competition.**
- Different approach to Bertrand, companies set quantities and than the price.
- **Assumptions:**
- Single market with homogeneous goods, two symmetric firms, demand: $Q = 1 - p$, $Q = q_1 + q_2$.

> If the companies are **symmetric**, then they face the same costs. This means the quantity (simultaneous moves) and price (both cases) will be equal.

- **Solve the problem:**
- *(1) Calculate the profit function of company 1.*
- $\pi_1 = (p - c) * q_1$
- *(2) Substitute the inverse demand function for p.*
- $\pi_1 = (1 - q_1 - q_2 - c) * q_1$
- *(3) Calculate the best respond function (foc of profit function with respect to strategic variable).*
- $\Pi_{q1} = -q_1 + 1 - q_1 - q_2 - c \iff q_1 = \frac{1}{2} * (1 - q_2 - c)$.

$\rightarrow$ Strategic substitutes because increasing amount of $q_2$ will decrease $q_1$.

- *(4) Calculate the equilibrium (inserting the best response functions into each other).*
- $q_1 = \frac{1}{2} * (1 - \frac{1}{2} * (1 - q_1 - c) - c) \rightarrow q_1 *. = \frac{1}{3} * (1 - c)$

$\rightarrow$ Optimal quantity for both companies because of the assumption of symmetry.

- *(5) Calculate the optimal price (with the inverse demand function).*
- $Q *. = \frac{2}{3} * (1 - c) p *. = 1 - \frac{2}{3} * (1 - c) = \frac{1+2c}{3}$
- This shows that companies will make a profit.
- *(6) Calculate the profit with optimal quantity and optimal price.*
- $\pi *. = \left(\frac{1+2c}{3} - c\right) * \left(\frac{1-c}{3}\right) = \frac{(1-c)^2}{9}$

- **Inverse demand and total welfare.**

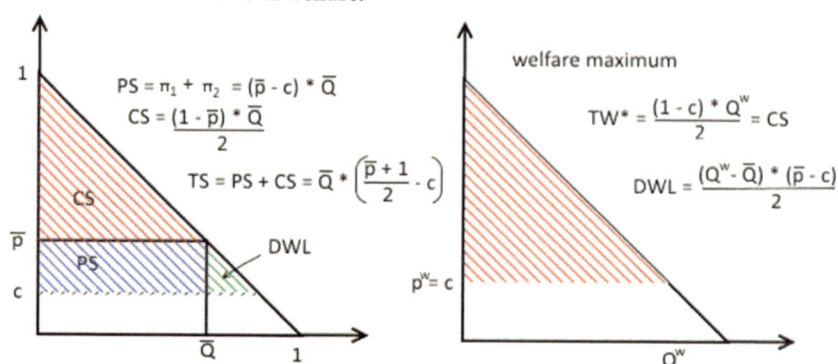

- Randomly choose a quantity and insert it into the inverse demand function to reveal the optimal price belonging to this quantity.
- Now you can calculate producers surplus (PS) and consumers surplus (CS) as well as the total surplus (TS) → TS is depended on the quantity chosen.
- Suppose we would know the optimal quantity, in this point the PS is zero.
- The dead-weight loss can be calculated and if it equals 0, the optimal quantity was found.

- **N-firm Cournot Oligopoly.**
- In the Cournot model the amount of companies in the market seems to be relevant (in contrast to Bertrand model), therefore we calculate the general quantity, price and profit with n firms.
- **Assumptions:**
- n firms in the market, homogeneous goods, $C_i = c * q_i$
- $inverse\ demand\ function: p = 1 - \sum_{j=1}^{n} q_j$
- **Guideline (same as before):**
- *(1+2) Calculate the profit function of company 1 with the inverse demand function for p.*
- $\pi_1 = (1 - \sum_{j=1}^{n} q_j - c) * q_1$
- *(3) Calculate the best respond function (f.o.c. of profit function with respect to strategic variable).*
- $\pi_{q1} = -q_1 + 1 - \sum_{j=1}^{n} q_j - c = 0\ because\ of\ symmetry\ \pi_{q1} = -q + 1 - n * q - c = 0$
- *(6) Calculate the profit with optimal quantity and optimal price.*
- $q*. = \frac{1-c}{n+1} Q*. = n * \left(\frac{1-c}{n+1}\right) p*. = 1 - n * \left(\frac{1-c}{n+1}\right) = \frac{1+nc}{n+1}$
- *(7) Calculate the equilibrium profits.*
- $\pi*. = \left(\frac{1+nc}{n+1} - c\right) * \left(\frac{1-c}{n+1}\right) = \left(\frac{1-c}{n+1}\right)^2 \lim n \to \infty \pi *. = 0$
=> Insensitivity of competition matters in the Cournot model.
- **Conclusions:**
- Companies have market power (can make profits).
- Increasing amount of companies will lower the mark-up of each other firm.
- If n goes to infinity we observe zero profits (→ pure competition).
- Cournot model is good because it has realistic result.
- Problem is that the assumptions don't hold: Firm don't chose quantities, they chose prices; prices don't "evolve" with the quantity.
→ A better model is existing which calculated the optimal capacity of firms and then the price, but this is not discussed here.

- **Cournot-Stackelberg model.**
- Firm 1 is Stackelberg leader, firm 2 Stackelberg follower, both are symmetric and compete in quantities (variation of Cournot example solved above).
  - (1) Calculate the best reaction function of the Stackelberg follower.
  - (2) Calculate the profit function of the Stackelberg leader and insert b.r.f. of S-follower.
  - (3) Derive profit function of S-leader to reveal optimal quantity.
  - (4) Calculate the optimal reaction of S-follower (its quantity).
  - (5) Find the prices for both companies (equal because of symmetry and homogeneous goods).
  - (6) Calculate the profit of both firms.
  - (7) Determine whether there is a first-mover advantage or not.

- (1) $q_2 = \frac{1 - q_1 - c}{2}$
- (2) $\pi_1 = q_1 * \left(1 - q_1 - \frac{1}{2} * (1 - q_1 - c) - c\right) = q_1 * \left(\frac{1}{2} - \frac{q_1}{2} - \frac{c}{2}\right)$
- (3) $\pi_{q1} = \frac{1}{2} - \frac{q_1}{2} - \frac{c}{2} - \frac{1}{2} * q_1 = 0 q_1 *. = \frac{1-c}{2}$
- (4) $q_2 *. = \frac{1}{2} * 1 - \frac{1-c}{2} - c = \frac{1-c}{4}$
- (5) $p *. = 1 - \left(\frac{1-c}{2}\right) - \left(\frac{1-c}{4}\right) = \frac{1+3c}{4}$
- (6) $\pi_1 *. = \left(\frac{1+3c}{4} - c\right) * \left(\frac{1-c}{2}\right) = \frac{(1-c)^2}{8}$

$\pi_2 *. = \left(\frac{1+3c}{4} - c\right) * \left(\frac{1-c}{4}\right) = \frac{(1-c)^2}{16}$

- (7) $\pi_{1seq} *. \frac{(1-c)^2}{8} > \pi_{1sim} *. \frac{(1-c)^2}{9}$ first mover advantage for S-leader.

$\pi_{2seq} *. \frac{(1-c)^2}{16} < \pi_{2sim} *. \frac{(1-c)^2}{9}$

- Firm 1 can set a relatively high quantity, firm 2 only a smaller quantity to not dilute prices and margins.

- **Bertrand Stackelberg with differentiated products (not in the exam).**
- The firms ate still symmetric and have no marginal costs.
- But now the products aren't homogeneous anymore, the demand doesn't only depend on the competitors price, but also from your own price.

→ Relationship between effect of your price and effect of competitors price is not equal, therefore differentiated products.

- $D_1 = 1 - \frac{2}{3} * p_1 + \frac{1}{3} * p_2 D_2 = 1 - \frac{2}{3} * p_2 + \frac{1}{3} * p_1$
- (1) Set up the best respond function for the S-follower.
- $\pi_2 = (p - MC) * D_2 = p_2 - \frac{2}{3} * p_2^2 + \frac{1}{3} * p_1 * p_2$
- $\pi_2' = 1 - \frac{4}{3} * p_2 + \frac{1}{3} * p_1 \rightarrow p_2 = \frac{3+p_1}{4}$
- Prices in this case are strategic complements, the higher firm 1 stets the price, the higher firm 2 will set it.
- (2) Insert the best respond function into the S-leader profit function and derive the optimal prices.
- $\pi_1 = p_1 - \frac{2}{3} * p_1^2 + \frac{1}{3} * \left(\frac{3+p_1}{4}\right) * p_1 = \left(\frac{15}{12} - \frac{7}{12} * p_1\right) * p_1$
- $\pi_1' = \frac{15}{12} - \frac{14}{12} * p_1 \rightarrow p_1 *. = \frac{15}{14} p_2 *. = \frac{3+\frac{15}{14}}{4} = \frac{57}{56}$
- (3) Calculate the optimal quantities by inserting the price into the respective demand function.
- $q_1 *. = 1 - \frac{5}{7} + \frac{19}{56} = \frac{5}{8} q_2 *. = 1 - \frac{19}{28} + \frac{5}{14} = \frac{19}{28}$
- (4) Calculate the respective profits.

- $\pi_1 *. = 0.67\pi_2 *. = 0.69 \rightarrow$ Second mover advantage in comparison to static games.
- **Summary of the four models.**
  ○ Bertrand and Cournot competition are important methods for the analysis of oligopolistic markets.
  ○ Bertrand Paradoxon: Bertrand competition implies high intensity of competition and reveals the same result as under perfect competition.
  ○ Cournot is competition in quantity, not in prices, and reveals more realistic outcomes.
  ○ Under Cournot-Stackelberg competition, the S-leader receives a first mover advantage.

- **Asymmetric Information and Market Failure.**
  ○ **Hidden information** (ex ante): Can't gather important information before the sign of a contract.
  · Market for used cars: Seller normally knows the quality of his cars, but buyer doesn't.
  · Averse selection is the extreme form and states, that only low-quality car sellers remain in market equilibrium => Question of how to solve this grievance.
  ○ **Hidden action (ex post)**: Can't control the behavior of contract partner, he has incentive to behave opportunistic.
  · The shareholders want the CEO to act in the interest of them, but only see the outcome of his work.
  · Principal induces agent to work hard, client satisfaction is only observable outcome.
  · CEO could use external factors to reach his compensation goals without great effort.
  => Question about an adequate labor contract.

- **Hidden Information – The Market for Used Cars.**
  ○ Suppose there could be three types of car sellers in the market, whose occurrence is equally likely and who have all the bargaining power (make only "take-it-or-leave-it" offers).

| Seller Types | Buyers Value | Sellers Cost | Sellers' Margins | Probability |
|---|---|---|---|---|
| high-quality | 12 | 9 | 3 | 1/3 |
| medium-quality | 6 | 4 | 2 | 1/3 |
| low-quality | 1 | 0 | 1 | 1/3 |

  ○ There is the objective function $U^B = E[v_i] - p$ where i = {H, M, L}.
  $\rightarrow$ Reveals the price the buyers are willing to pay with respect to the types of cars available in the market.
  ○ Sellers only stay in the market if they meet their costs.
  ○ Possible outcomes are $S_1 = \{H, M, L\}$, $S_2 = \{M, L\}$, $S_3 = \{L\}$, $S_4 = \{H, M\}$, $S_5 = \{H, L\}$.
  ○ **Show which of these outcomes constitutes an equilibrium.**
  · $S_1$ : E [v | S = $S_1$] = 1/3 * 12 + 1/3 * 6 + 1/3 * 1 = 19/3
  · Because 19/3 < 9 high-quality sellers can't meet their costs and won't stay in the market.
  $\rightarrow$ No equilibrium.
  · $S_2$ : E [v | S = $S_2$] = ½ * 6 + ½ * 1 = 3.5
  · Because 3.5 < 4 medium-quality sellers can't meet their costs and won't stay in the market.
  $\rightarrow$ No equilibrium.
  · $S_3$ : E [v | S = $S_3$] = 1 * 1 = 1
  · Because 1 < 0 low-quality sellers can meet their costs.
  $\rightarrow$ $S^* = S_3$ with the respective price $p^* = 1$
  · $S_4$ : E [v | S = $S_4$] = ½ * 12 + ½ * 6 = 9
  · High-quality sellers can just break-even and will stay in the market; $S_4$ could be an equilibrium with $p^* = 9$
  · $S_4$ requires strict absence of low-quality sellers, but they will enter the market and dilute prices.

→ No equilibrium.
- $S_5 : E [v \mid S = S_5] = \frac{1}{2} * 12 + \frac{1}{2} * 1 = 6.5$
- Because $6.5 < 9$ high-quality sellers can't meet their costs and won't stay in the market.
→ No equilibrium.

- **Different example with unknown probability.**

| Seller Types | Buyers Value | Sellers Cost | Sellers' Margins | Probability |
|---|---|---|---|---|
| high-quality | 10 | 9 | 1 | $\frac{1}{2}$ |
| medium-quality | 5 | 4 | 1 | $(\frac{1}{2} - x)$ |
| low-quality | 4 | 3 | 1 | $x$ |

- **Prove whether $S_1$ or $S_2$ is an equilibrium.**
- $S_1 : E [v \mid S = S_1] = \frac{1}{2} * 10 + (\frac{1}{2} - x) * 5 + x * 4 < 9 \quad \rightarrow \quad x < -3/2$
- Because negative probability can't occur, $S_1$ is no equilibrium.
- $S_2 : E[v \mid S = S_2] = \frac{\frac{1}{2}-x}{\frac{1}{2}-x+x} * 5 + \frac{x}{\frac{1}{2}-x+x} * 4 = 2 * \left(\frac{1}{2} - x\right) * 5 + 2x * 4 \le 4$
- Because only two seller-types are in the market, the total probability now is prob 1 + prob 2 and the respective probabilities must be divided through this.
- Prob 1 + prob 2 aren't 100% but in this ratio they reveal the correct probabilities.
=> **Equilibrium if $x \le \frac{1}{2}$.**

- **Welfare implications of adverse selection.**
- Adverse selection leads to a total / partial market break-down (equilibrium consists only of bad products).
- Seller only realize margins of 1 (example above), but could realize margins of 3 without making any individual worse-off → Gains are left unexploited.
=> Averse selection is Pareto inefficient.
- The market is not totally separated, is incomplete.

- **Tries to (partially) solve the problem of adverse selection.**
- **Screening**: Buyer can gather as much information as she can, e.g. verification by independent experts.
- **Signaling**: High-quality sellers have (i) high enough margins and (ii) best quality to set up a special warranty which other seller-types can't set up (profitably).
→ High-quality sellers could set themselves apart from the market.
=> Helps to yield a better market outcome.

- **Further examples for adverse selection.**
- **Insurance markets.**
- People know their individual health better, insurance companies not.
- Healthy people are more likely to cancel the insurance when company must raise the prices because of the unhealthy people who lied to get the insurance and are more expensive.
- *Averse selection*: Only unhealthy clients remain in the insurance and pay high fees.
- Solutions could be mandatory insurances.
- **Credit markets.**
- Borrowers know their individual credit risk, the bank doesn't.
- Lending money to "bad-borrowers" will increase costs and therefore interest rates.
- People with good credit rate won't take this high interest rates and search for other institutions.
- *Adverse selection*: Only borrowers with high credit risk are loan takers with high interest.
- Possible solution could be the usage of computerized credit histories.

- **Hidden Action.**
- Principal hires an agent to perform a certain task, but can only observe the outcome.
- Labor contract should not be related to outcome because the real effort of the employee is not the only factor of success.
- Moral hazard arises if the employee doesn't feel observed enough.
- **Example: Sales Agent.**
- Total sales per sale agent depends on effort and external effects, but company wants to induce employees to work hard.
- Sales Agent as no other source of income and like stable income.
- **Compensation of the sales agent.**
- In case of no sales she will receive $\pi_L = 0$, medium sales $\pi_M = 100$, high sales $\pi_H = 400$.
- Related to the effort of the sales agent (high or low), the probabilities of occurrence for the related amounts of sales is given by the following table.

| Agent's effort (e) | Prob ($\pi = \pi_L$) | Prob ($\pi = \pi_M$) | Prob ($\pi = \pi_H$) | E [$\pi$ \| e] |
|---|---|---|---|---|
| high | 0.1 | 0.3 | 0.6 | X |
| low | 0.6 | 0.3 | 0.1 | Y |

- Calculate the **expected compensation** for each level of effort.
- $X = E[\pi \mid e = H] = 0.1 * 0 + 0.3 * 100 + 0.6 * 400 = 270$
- $Y = E[\pi \mid e = L] = 0.6 * 0 + 0.3 * 100 + 0.1 * 400 = 70$
- The individual utility function of the sales agent is given by $U_A(w, e) = \sqrt{w} - ee = \{0, 5\}$
- The sales agent are offered two different contracts.
- (I) getting $w_1$ with probability $p_1$ and $w_2$ with probability $(1 - p_1)$.
- (II) getting $E = [w_1 * p_1 + w_2 * (1 - p_1)]$.
→ Suppose the sales agent is risk averse, which contract will she choose?
- Expected value of (I) and (II) are the same, but regarding the utility function of the sales agent we can calculate the utility received.
- $p_1 = 0.4$, $w_1 = 4$, $w_2 = 16$
- $U_I = 0.4 * \sqrt{4} + 0.6 * \sqrt{16} = 3.2$
- $E_{II} = 0.4 * 4 + 0.6 * 16 = 11.2 U_{II} = \sqrt{11.2} \approx 3.3466$
=> Utility of (II) is higher because of certainty, therefore prefer (II).
- This result is related to the risk aversion of the sales agent, a behavior often observed in reality.

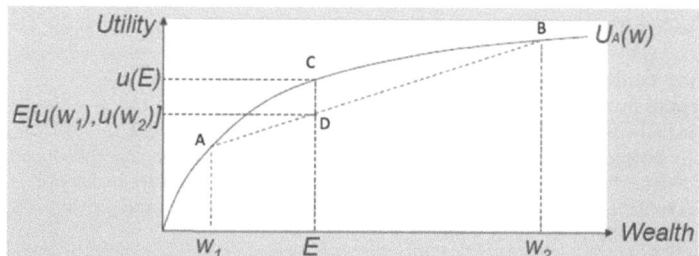

- Concave utility functions means decreasing marginal utility, means risk aversion.
- In case of a risk loving agent, the utility function is convex and has increasing marginal utility.
- And a risk neutral agent has a linear utility function and is indifferent in choosing contract I or II.

- **Modeling the right contract.**
- There is a trade-off between insurance and incentive.
- Insurance: Offer the agent certain payments because she prefers them.
- Incentive: Incentivize the agent to work hard.
- Suppose there are **symmetric information**, than the optimal wage for the agent to just meet her reservation utility will be 196 with a related profit for the principal of $270 - 196 = 74$.

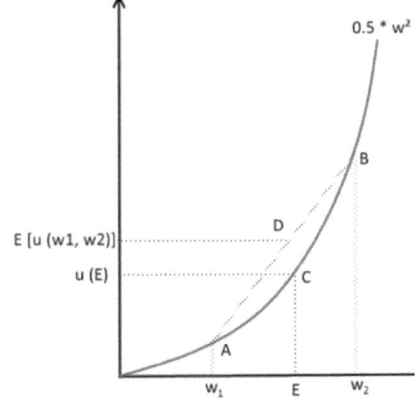

$$\sqrt{w} - 5 \geq 9 \leftrightarrow w \geq (9+5)^2 = 196 < 270$$

- Come back to the more realistic assumption of **asymmetric information**.
- If the principal would offer the agent a wage of 196, a rational agent would spend no effort and the "profit" of the principal will become a loss ($\pi = 70 - 196 = -126$).
- If paying an adequate wage for spending no effort, there will also be a loss (adequate wage according the approach from above $w = 81$; $\pi = 70 - 81 = -11$).
=> Principal must induce the agent to work hard.
- **Benchmark Case: A risk neutral agent.**
- $U = w - e$    $e = \{0, 25\}$    reservation utility $= 81$
- Optimal contract would be a franchise contract: Paying a fee before each month to receive the right to receive all profits.
- Optimal fee then would be   $81 = 270 - 25 - X$    $X = 164$.
→ With a monthly fee of 164 the risk-neutral agent would accept the franchise contract.
=> Turn the agent into his own principal to solve the problem of asymmetric information.
- **Modeling the right contract for the risk-averse agent.**
- The principal faces two constraints.
- (1) Voluntary participation: If the offer is too little, the agent will refuse the contract.
- Salary must at least equal the reservation utility → U (e) ≥ reservation utility.
→ It must be profitable for the agent to accept.
- (2) Incentive compatibility: Payoffs must be structured in a way that working hard provides a greater utility than shirking.
- U (e = h) ≥ U (e = l), incentivize the agent to work hard.
=> Minimization problem with two constraints.
- To solve this minimization problem, set up the Lagrangian with the two constraints and solve it.
→ In the exam we will only get two possible events for the utility function (low sales and high sales, no medium) so setting up the Lagrangian won't be needed; the two constraints can simply be inserted into each other and the utility function to reveal the optimal wages for each situation (sales amount).
- **Binding Constraints.**
- **Participation constraint**: If not binding, than lowering the wage will have the same result, but saves the principal money.
- **Incentive constraint**: If not binding, than lowering the wage would have the same result, but saves the principal money.

- **Welfare Loss.**
- A welfare loss occurs because the agent has to bear some risk.
- The first best (efficient outcome, maximizing social welfare) is the franchise contract, but only possible under symmetric information.

- In this case the wage is w = 196 and the expected profit for the principal $\pi = 74 + 9 = 83$.
- In case of asymmetric information, the optimal salary must be higher to incentivize the agent to work harder, therefore w = 204, 57 and expected profit $\pi = 65.43 + 9 = 74.43$.
- The total welfare loss can be expressed as the loss for the principal DWL = 83 – 74, 43 = 8.57.

=> If there is a technology enabling the principal to perfectly monitor the agent, she would be willing to pay 8.57 to receive this.

- **Conclusions – Hidden Action.**
  - Hidden action leads to moral hazard because wrong behavior can't be sanctionated.
  - Principal must incentivize the agent to work hard, which can be very expensive.
  - Most often the degree of insurance of the agent is limited.

=> Basic trade-off between insurance and incentive.

- **Conclusions – Asymmetric Information.**
  - Asymmetric information is like a sequential game, we're searching for the subgame perfect equilibrium.
  - Only one player has relevant information determining an optimal contract.
  - Before the contract is signed, hidden information could lead to averse selection.
  - After the contract is signed, hidden action could lead to moral hazard.

- **Externalities – The Heating Game.**
  - Suppose there is building with 5 similar flats and rational inhabitants.
  - The total heating cost for each flat can be measured, but not the heating cost of each bathroom.

→ These costs are split equally between the inhabitants.

- Therefore the cost functions are $C_i = \frac{\sum_j x_j * c}{5}$ and the utility functions $U_i = \sqrt{x_i} - C_i$
- Question is about the optimal amount of heating in the bathroom and the rational.
- **Optimal amount of heating.**
- Use the cost function and solve the minimization problem.
- Social welfare = $\sum_{i=1}^{5} \sqrt{x_i} - c * x_i$ efficiency requires $x_1 = x_2 = x_3 = x_4 = x_5 = x$
- $SW = 5 * \sqrt{x} - 5 * c * x$ $SW_x = \frac{\frac{5}{2}*1}{\sqrt{x}} - 5 * c = 0 <=> x = \frac{1}{4*c^2}$

=> The optimal amount of heating would be $1 / (4 * c^2)$.

- **Rational amount of heating // market outcome.**
- Use the utility function and solve the maximization problem.
- $U_1 = \sqrt{x_1} - \frac{c*(x_1+x_2+x_3+x_4+x_5)}{5}$
- $(U_1)_{x_1} = \frac{1}{2*\sqrt{x_1}} - \frac{c}{5} = 0 <=>$

$\sqrt{x_1} = \frac{5}{2c} <=> x = \frac{25}{4*c^2}$

=> Individual rational amount of heating is 25 times higher than the efficient outcome.

- **Externalities:** Effect of economic behavior which is not reflected in the price.
- **Internalization of externalities:** Take the social costs into account.
- **Effects of internalization of a negative externality like pollution.**
- The steel industry is well-known to face high pollution, is a negative externality.

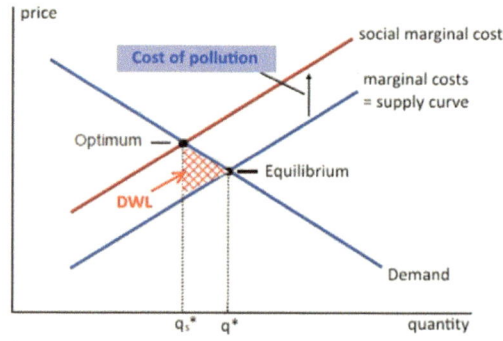

16

- When taking the social costs into account, the socially efficient quantity is lower and the socially efficient price is higher.
- Marginal costs (= supply curve) will be turned into social marginal costs and a dead-weight loss will be revealed.
- **Effects of internalization of positive externalities like education.**
- Education is a classical example.
- The demand function is extended by the marginal external benefit (MEB) and reveals the marginal social benefit (MSB).
- After this adjustment the DWL will become visible.
→ Solution could be to subsidize the education industry.

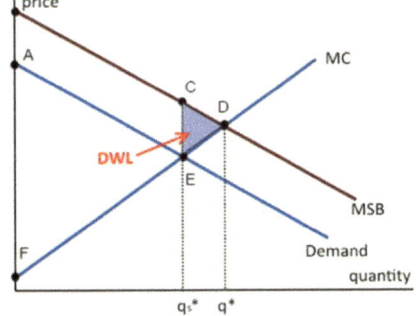

- **External effects and efficiency.**
- Economic subjects don't use the "right" price signals, the social costs / benefits aren't considered.
- In case of negative externalities the private costs are lower than the social ones, so too much of the goods are consumed.
- In case of positive externalities the private gain is lower than the social one, so too few of the good is consumed.
- First welfare theorem states that only a competitive equilibrium is Pareto efficient.

- **Externalities and companies' perspective.**
- If the government sanctionate negative externalities, there is an optimal point for each company revealing the best ratio between abatement costs and benefits.
- The marginal costs of avoidance (reduce the production) must equal the marginal benefit of avoidance (avoid costs of illness).
=> Classical trade-off of governments; harming the economy or the nature?

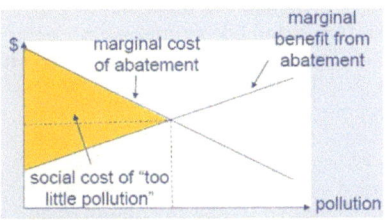

- **Government instruments of internalizing externalities.**
- (1) *Legal limits* (emission standards): Ceiling on quantity of pollution.
- (2) *Pigouvian tax* (eco tax): For each unit of pollution, a tax has to be paid.
- (3) *Tradeable emission allowance* (green certificates): Needing more certificates to pollute more.

- **Comparing the legal limit with the pigouvian tax.**
- Suppose two companies equally generate a pollution of 10, but company A is more efficient than company B and has therefore lower abatement costs.
- (1) The government issued every producer to cut pollution to the half (legal limit).
- (2) The government levies a pigouvian tax amounted at $ 3.

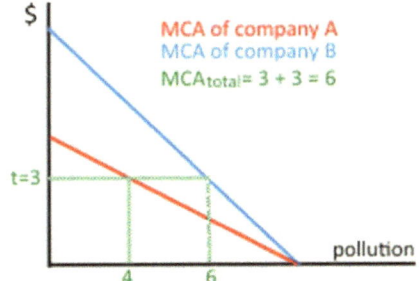

→ Under assumption of full information.

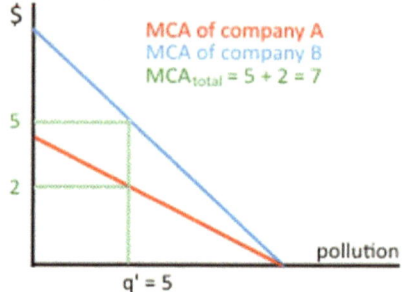

- In both cases the total pollution is reduced by the half, but the pigouvian tax has minimized the marginal costs of abatement for both companies.
→ Legal limits are less efficient than pigouvian taxes because MCA differ between firms.
=> Furthermore there is a welfare gain if preferring pigouvian taxes over legal limits.

- **Tradeable emission allowances.**
- Government fixes the quantity of pollution by emitting certificated rights to pollute a certain amount; will provide a very efficient outcome.
- Certificates can be traded on "stock" markets and in perfect competition, the market price will equal the marginal costs for abatement of the firms.
- Initial distribution isn't important for an efficient outcome, but for a fair one.
- **Grandfathering**: Each firm receives certificates for free related to the amount of pollution in the last year and can sell them if becoming more efficient, or buy new ones if expanding.
- **Auction**: All firms start with zero certificates and buy the amount needed from the state.
=> In this simplified setting we neglect trading costs and fraud.
- **Comparison of tradeable emission allowance and pigouvian tax.**
- When the government has *complete information*, a pigouvian tax is equally efficient as a TEA.
→ Marginal costs of abatement will equal marginal benefit of abatement.
- Under *incomplete information* the efficiency of both methods can't be predicted this easy.
- Pigouvian taxes (i) reduce the uncertainty of firms and (ii) allows the calculation of costs, but (iii) the total amount of pollution can only be estimated.

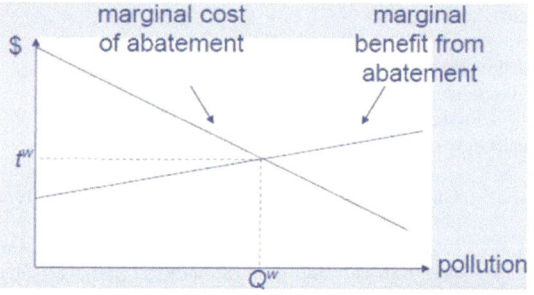

- TEA (i) will set an upper-limit for pollution, but (ii) don't allow a reliable estimation of costs for the firms.

- **The Coase Theorem.**
- Steel industry example from before.
- The local steel industry (perfect competition) pollutes the river and harms the local fisher.
- Problem is that the property rights of the river aren't defined clearly.
- Suppose the fisher "owns" the river, than the companies must pay a fee to compensate his gone profits if they want to keep on polluting.
- If the company has the right to pollute, the fisherman will pay a fee amounted at the abatement costs of the companies to prevent pollution.

=> Even though the internalization of (negative) externalities is possible under clearly defined property rights, the outcome must not be always fair.

- **Requirements of the Coase Theorem.**
- Clearly defined property rights (allocation is irrelevant for efficiency, only for fairness).
- Symmetric information.
- No negotiation costs.

=> Then the market will always come up with efficient ways to internalize externalities.

- **Problems with the Coase Theorem.**
- In reality property rights aren't clearly defined and pollution can't be measured.
- Negotiation, tries to measure pollution and information is very expensive.
- The number of humans involved / affected can't be foreseen.
- Fairness isn't considered in this theorem, but in the law.
- Dynamic incentive effects: When receiving a fee for stopping pollution, the company will increase pollution because the other party is dependent on no pollution.

- **Public Goods.**
- Two characteristics of public goods: **rivalry** (does the consumption of one human influences the consumption of another one) and **excludability** (does the consumption of one human excludes the consumption of another one).
- *Private goods* like a jeans can only be worn by one human and buying it, makes it unaffordable for others.
- *Allmende* goods are matural resouces because you can't prevent humans to take them, but taking them will reduce the amount remaining for other humans.

|  | rival | non-rival |
|---|---|---|
| excludable | Private Goods<br>Cars | Club Goods<br>Public Transport[1] |
| non-excludable | Common Goods<br>("Allmende Goods")<br>Ocean fish | Public Goods<br>Lighthouse |

- *Club goods* are goods like Pay-TV for which non-paying humans can be excluded, but the amount of buyers doesn't influence each other.
- *Public goods (s.str.)* are goods like national defense for which humans can't be excluded and which aren't rival at all.
- **Public goods lead to market failure.**
- **Public goods (s.str.) won't be provided by** the market because of non-excludability; they can't generate revenue because of the free-rider problem.

|  |  | B | |
|---|---|---|---|
|  |  | provide | don't |
| A | provide | (0.3,0.3) | (-0.4,1) |
|  | don't | (1,-0.4) | (0,0) |

- Just make a static game out of this problem: Suppose communities A and B could build a lighthouse for 1,4 and will benefit by 1. If they share costs equally they will receive a welfare surplus of 0,3 each. If only one community pays for the building, it will face a loss, but the other community will benefit even more.

=> Nash equilibrium reveals that optimal choice is not to provide the lighthouse.

- **Club goods** can be provided, but only in an inefficient way.

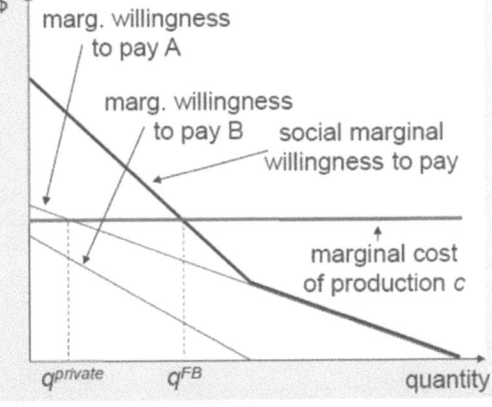

- The marginal costs for providing this good to another user are zero, but consumers with positive willingness to pay won't use them because of the fixed price.
  - Consumer B has a positive willingness to pay which is below the fixed costs of the club good. Therefore she won't consume the good even though the provider would make a profit when lowering the price for her.
→ Problem of asymmetric information.
- Vertical aggregation of demand (to social marginal willingness to pay) would be efficient, but isn't that easy to implement in reality.
=> **Because of this market failures the government has to intervene.**
  - **Financing of public goods.**
  - Public goods (s.str.) have to be financed by the government because of the tax authority.
  - Club goods can be financed by private companies, but the result isn't that efficient.


- **Summary of externalities and public goods.**
  - Externalities are effects of economic action to the benefit (positive ones) / disadvantage (negative ones) of other market participants and aren't reflected in the market price.
→ Negative externalities lead to an excessive usage.
- Public goods are non-rival and non-excludable and therefore can only be provided by the government.
  - Private companies will under-provide the market with club goods.
  - Externalities and public goods lead to market failure and justify government intervention.


- **Pure Exchange Economy.**
  - Two different consumers with exogenously given quantities of two goods bananas B and coconut C.
  - Set up the edgeworth box for both consumers to reveal all feasible ways to allocate the two goods between the two players R and F.
  - Player R starts with the consumption bundle (8, 2) and player F with (2, 8) (bananas,

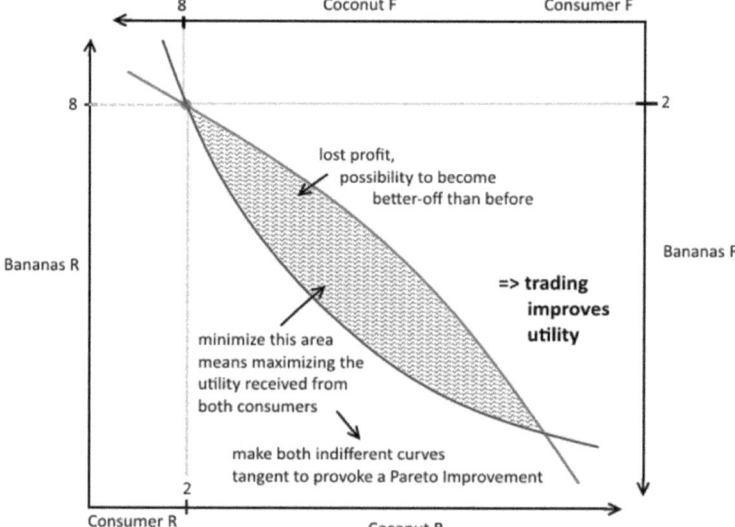

coconut).
- Shift the red indifference curve (from player F) closer to the origin of player R will make her better of (& v.v.).

- Minimizing the green area means maximizing the utility received from both players and increase the efficiency from the market allocation.
- Initial starting point determines the optimal consumption bundle for both players (= the tangency point of both indifference curves).
→ Plotting all possible optimal points into a graph reveals the **contract curve**.
- Contract curve reveals the optimal points for both players, but there are several possible points within the area to make at least one player better-off.
- Points B and C are the limit of the area for optimal consumption bundles, in this points one player will become better-off whereas the other one stays as good as before.
- Problem is that efficient outcome isn't always fair, therefore move the initial starting point into the middle to let the utilities received from each consumption bundle converge together.

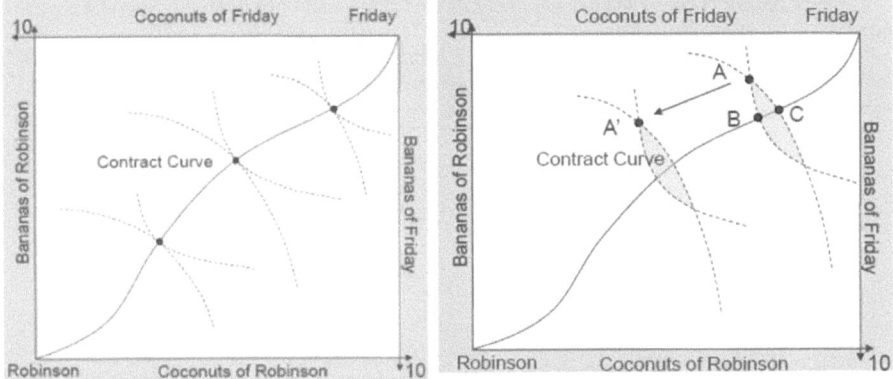

- The contract curve can be turned into a utility frontier, a comparison of utility received by R and F → Question whether the distribution is "good" or not arises.

## Contract Curve          Utility Frontier

- **Welfare functions to determine whether a distribution is "good" or not.**
- Economics only reveals efficient outcomes, not fair, just or "good" ones.
- Utility is an ordinal concept and can hardly be compared with each other.
=> **Social welfare functions** are a tool judge efficient outcomes.
- **Two kinds of welfare functions.**
- **Utilitarian:** The total welfare is the sum of each individuals welfare.
- Problem is that when the rich ones become even richer, total welfare will increase.

=> Concept doesn't take justice / fairness into account.
- **Rawls:** Total welfare is determined by the lowest welfare one player gains.
- Total welfare equals the lowest welfare available multiplied with the total number of participants. → Same idea as with perfect complements.

- **Competitive Equilibrium.**
- Equilibrium characterized by market clearing in which all participants maximize their objective functions with the given prices.
- Price taking behavior: Participants as price takers, no market power.
- **Market clearing.**
- No excesses available (excessive demand or supply).
- Set prices for coconut and banana in our initial example and just randomly suppose a price ratio of 3:1 (coconut to banana).
- Furthermore suppose that R wants to sell 3 bananas and F wants to sell 2 coconut; both will use the capital received to buy the other good to increase their utility.

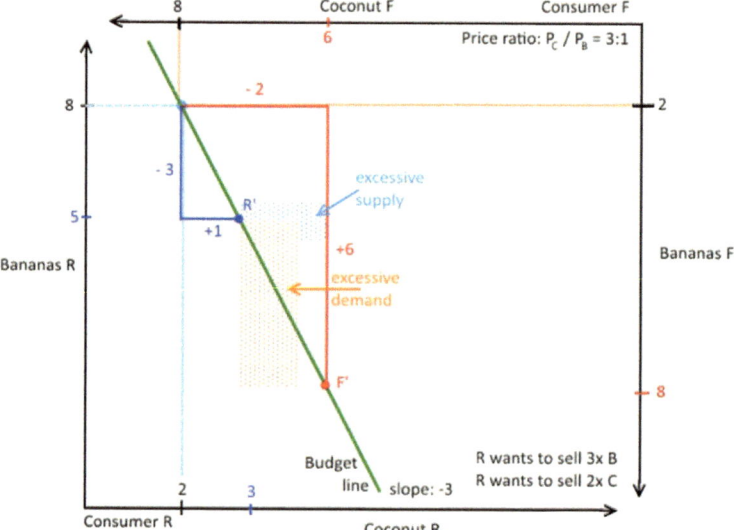

→ No market clearing because of the excessive demand and supply.
=> Solve this problem by adjusting the prices (assumption that we are a social planner).

22

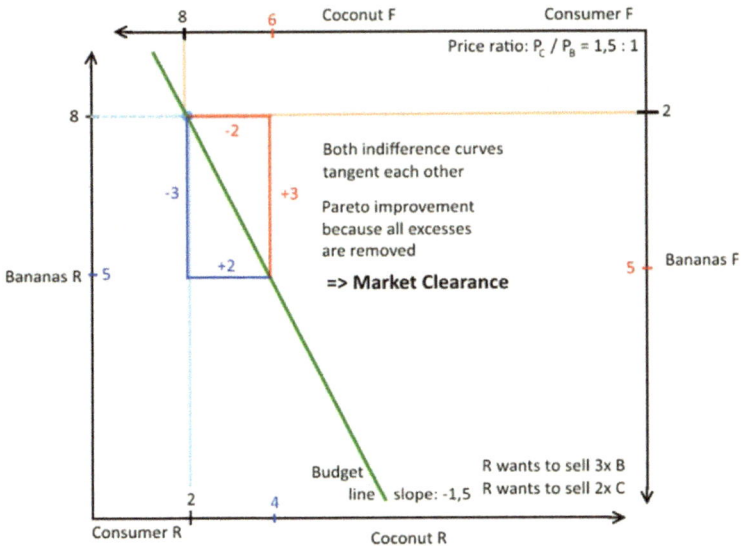

- **First Fundamental Theorem of Welfare Economics.**
- A competitive equilibrium is always / has always to be Pareto efficient.
- Marginal rate of substitution MRS equals the relative prices (slope of the budget line).
- In case of two players, the MRS of player one should equal the MRS of player 2 to generate a Pareto efficient outcome.
- **Interpretation.**
- Competitive markets ensure Pareto-efficiency.
- Mechanism works with little information (own preferences, market price).
- Formalization of the invisible hand by Adam Smith.
- **Key assumptions** are: No market power, no externalities, no asymmetric information.

- **Second Fundamental Theorem of Welfare Economics.**
- If we want to receive a fairer optimal outcome, we don't have to change prices or quantities, only the initial distribution. → No need to give up efficiency.
- **Interpretation.**
- We can implement every desired distribution by only redistribute the initial wealth.
- Social planner can only implement desired outcome when knowing preferences, but then would directly implement the best situation.
=> No need to change prices or quantities, only change initial distribution of wealth.

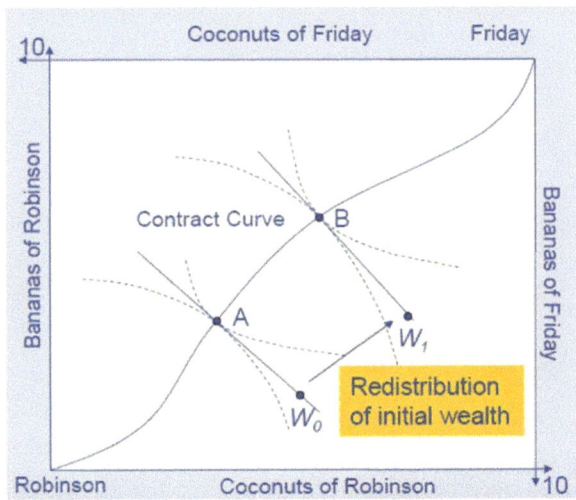

- **Important assumption**: Redistribution is possible without any distortion effects (poll tax, lump sum transfers).

- **Summary of Competitive Equilibrium.**
- Pareto efficient outcomes are most often declared as "good" or just.
- Competitive markets are the best way to implement Pareto efficient outcomes.